D1573362

Bird Illustrations
CD-ROM and Book

DOVER PUBLICATIONS, INC.
Mineola, New York

The CD-ROM on the inside back cover contains all of the images shown in the book. There is no installation necessary. Just insert the CD into your computer and call the images into your favorite software (refer to the documentation with your software for further instructions). Each image has been scanned at 600 dpi and saved in six different formats—BMP, EPS, GIF, JPEG, PICT, and TIFF. The JPEG and GIF files—the most popular graphics file types used on the Web—are Internet-ready.

The "Images" folder on the CD contains a number of different folders. All of the TIFF images have been placed in one folder, as have all of the PICT, all of the EPS, etc. The images in each of these folders are identical except for file format. Every image has a unique file name in the following format: xxx.xxx. The first 3 or 4 characters of the file name, before the period, correspond to the number printed with the image in the book. The last 3 characters of the file name, after the period, refer to the file format. So, 001.TIF would be the first file in the TIFF folder.

Also included on the CD-ROM is Dover Design Manager, a simple graphics editing program for Windows that will allow you to view, print, crop, and rotate the images.

For technical support, contact:
  Telephone: 1 (617) 249-0245
  Fax: 1 (617) 249-0245
  Email: dover@artimaging.com
  Internet: **http://www.dovertechsupport.com**
The fastest way to receive technical support is via email or the Internet.

Sources of the Illustrations

50 Favorite Birds Coloring Book, Lisa Bonforte, copyright © 1982 by Lisa Bonforte. *Audubon's Birds of America Coloring Book,* Paul E. Kennedy, copyright © 1974 by Dover Publications, Inc. *Birds of Prey Coloring Book,* John Green, copyright © 1989 by John Green. *State Birds and Flowers Coloring Book,* Annika Bernhard, copyright © 1990 by Annika Bernhard. *Hawaiian Plants and Animals Coloring Book,* Y. S. Green, copyright © 1999 by Dover Publications, Inc. *Sea and Shore Birds Coloring Book,* Ruth Soffer, copyright © 1999 by Ruth Soffer. *Arctic and Antarctic Life Coloring Book,* Ruth Soffer, copyright © 1998 by Dover Publications, Inc. *North American Ducks, Geese and Swans Coloring Book,* Ruth Soffer, copyright © 1996 by Ruth Soffer. *Swampland Animals Coloring Book,* Ruth Soffer, copyright © 1997 by Dover Publications, Inc. *Tropical Birds Coloring Book,* Lucia de Leiris, copyright © 1984 by Lucia de Leiris. *Long Island Nature Preserves Coloring Book,* Sy and Dot Barlowe, copyright © 1997 by Dover Publications, Inc. *Zoo Animals Coloring Book,* Jan Sovak, copyright © 1993 by Dover Publications, Inc. *Backyard Nature Coloring Book,* Dot Barlowe, copyright © 1999 by Dorothea Barlowe. *Rain Forest Coloring Book,* Annika Bernhard, copyright © 1998 by Annika Bernhard. *Nocturnal Creatures Coloring Book,* Ruth Soffer, copyright © 1998 by Ruth Soffer. *African Plains Coloring Book,* Dianne Gaspas-Ettl, copyright © 1996 by Dover Publications, Inc. *North American Desert Life Coloring Book,* Ruth Soffer, copyright © 1994 by Dover Publications, Inc.

Bibliographical Note

Bird Illustrations CD-ROM and Book, first published in 2005, contains a new selection of images from *Big Book of Bird Illustrations,* selected and arranged by Maggie Kate, first published by Dover Publications, Inc., in 2001, which is, in turn, a selection of illustrations from previously published Dover books and other sources.

Dover Electronic Clip Art®

International Standard Book Number: 0-486-99669-7

Manufactured in the United States of America
Dover Publications, Inc., 31 East 2nd Street, Mineola, N.Y. 11501

CONTENTS

Common Grackle
001

Mourning Dove
002

Ruby-Throated
Hummingbird
004

Northern Bobwhite
003

005
Starling

Eastern
Wood Pewee
006

House Wren
007

Red-Eyed
Vireo
008

Towhee
009

Wood Thrush
010

011
Eastern Bluebird

Red-Headed
Woodpecker
012

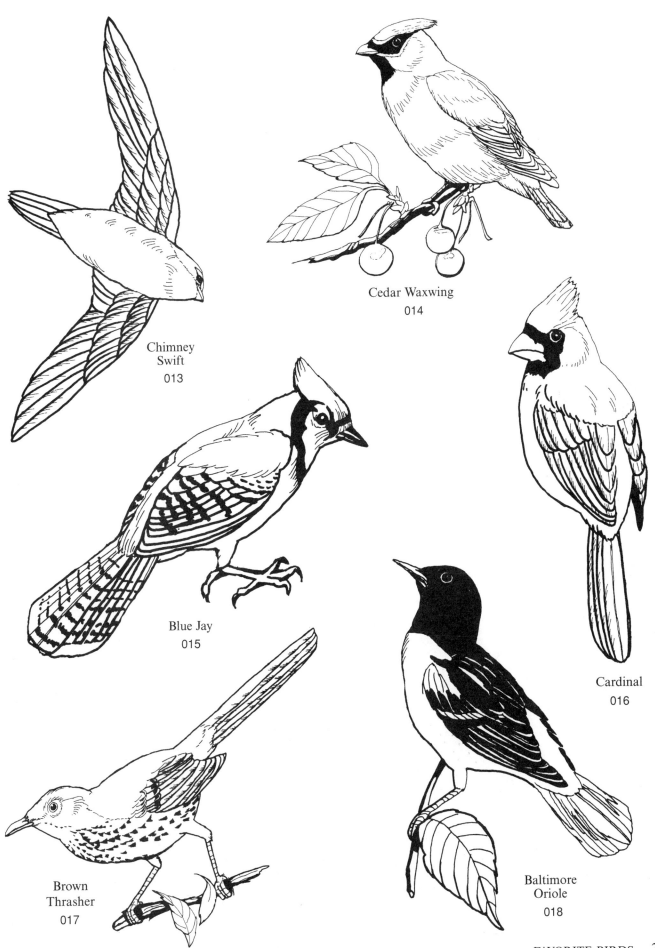

Chimney
Swift
013

Cedar Waxwing
014

Blue Jay
015

Cardinal
016

Brown
Thrasher
017

Baltimore
Oriole
018

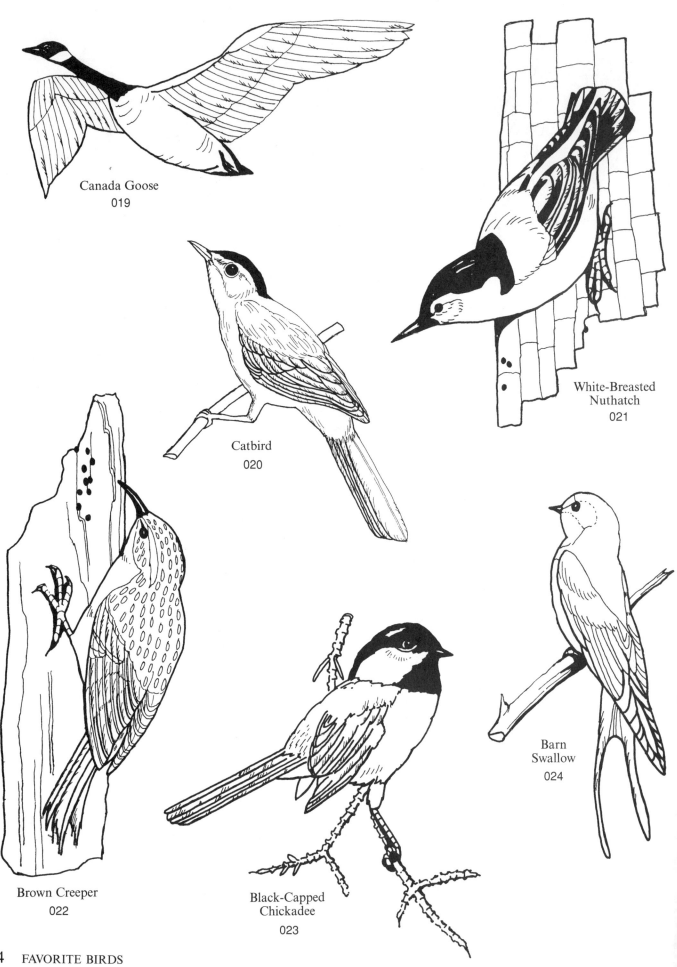

Canada Goose
019

Catbird
020

White-Breasted
Nuthatch
021

Brown Creeper
022

Black-Capped
Chickadee
023

Barn
Swallow
024

Nighthawk
025

Slate-Colored Junco
026

Mallard
028

Sparrowhawk
027

Tufted Titmouse
029

Robin
030

FAVORITE BIRDS   5

Pigeon
031

Herring Gull
032

Song Sparrow
033

Red-Winged
Blackbird
034

White-Crowned
Sparrow
035

Common
Yellowthroat
036

Goldfinch
037

Yellow-Shafted
Flicker
038

Common
Crow
039

Cowbird
040

Green Heron
041

House Sparrow
042

Northern Mockingbird
043

Killdeer
044

Downy
Woodpecker
045

Yellow Warbler
046

Purple
Martin
047

Chipping
Sparrow
048

Myrtle Warbler
049

Purple
Finch
050

Snowy
Owl
052

Belted
Kingfisher
051

White-Throated
Sparrow
053

Canada Warbler
054

Scarlet Tanager
055

056

American
Redstart

Painted Bunting
058

Robin
057

Horned Lark
059

060

Snowy Egret

Whippoorwill
061

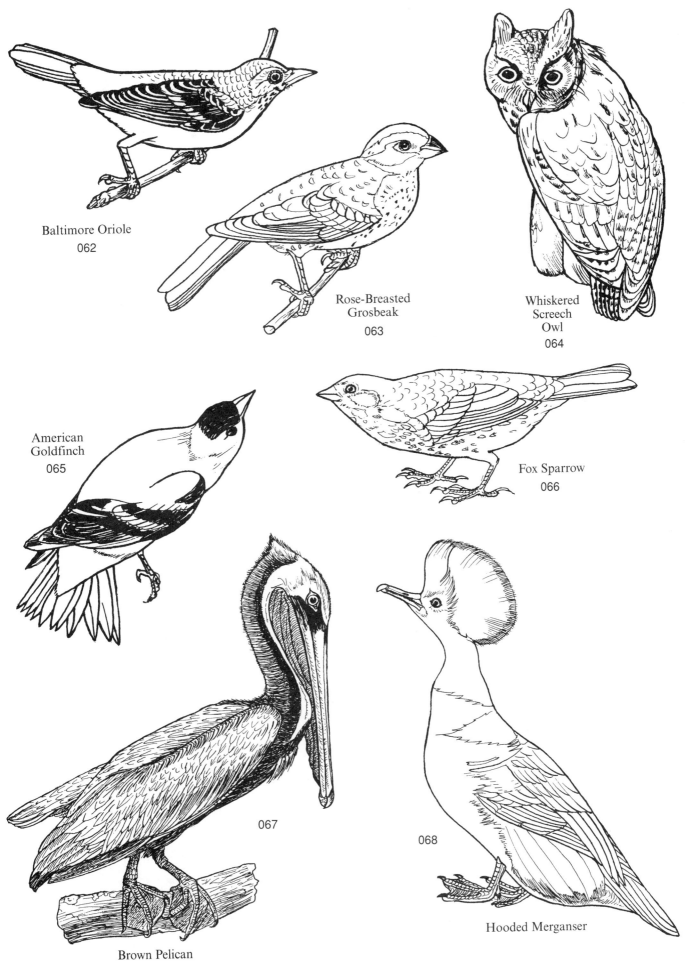

Baltimore Oriole
062

Rose-Breasted
Grosbeak
063

Whiskered
Screech
Owl
064

American
Goldfinch
065

Fox Sparrow
066

067

068

Brown Pelican

Hooded Merganser

Eastern
Bluebird
069

Ruby-Throated
Hummingbird
070

Cardinal
071

Great Blue
Heron
072

Eastern Meadowlark
073

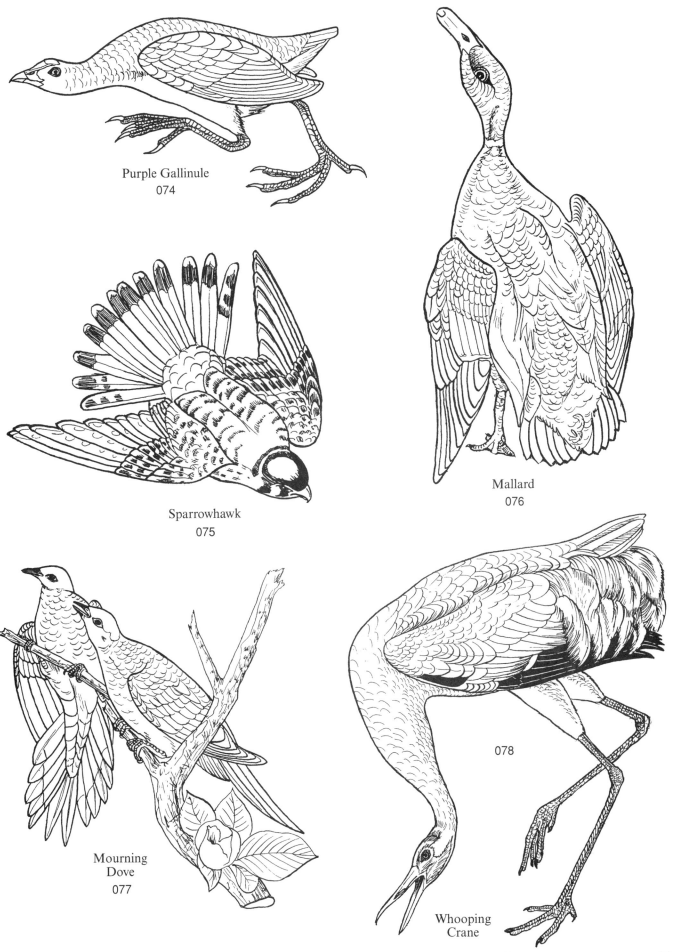

Purple Gallinule
074

Sparrowhawk
075

Mallard
076

Mourning
Dove
077

078

Whooping
Crane

Yellow-Breasted
Chat
079

Evening
Grosbeak
080

Rufous-Sided
Towhee
081

Blue Jay
082

083

Blackburnian
Warbler
084

Wild Turkey

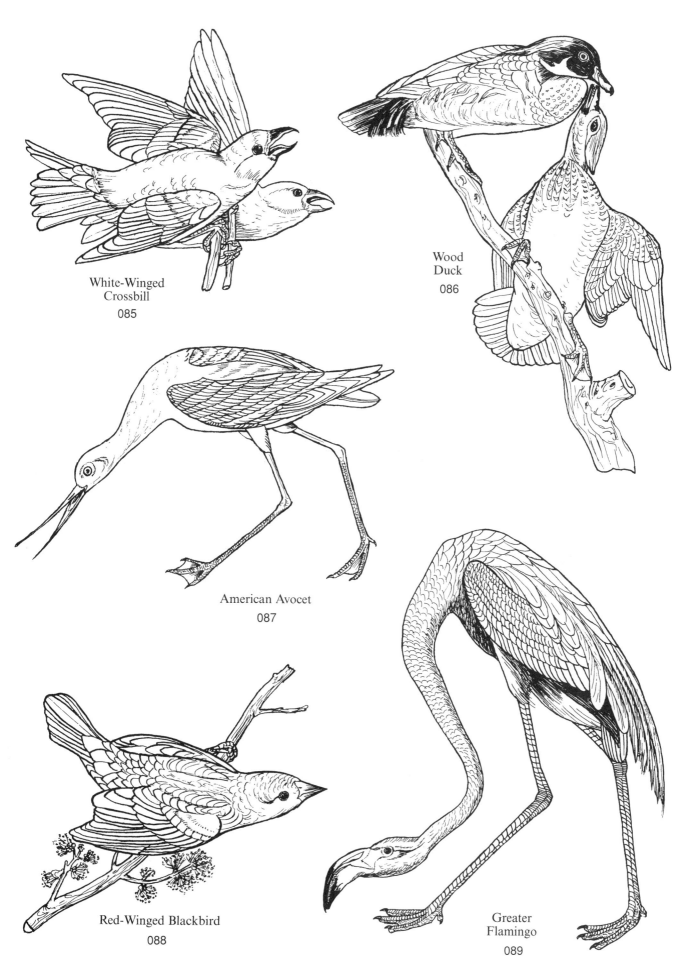

White-Winged
Crossbill
085

Wood
Duck
086

American Avocet
087

Red-Winged Blackbird
088

Greater
Flamingo
089

Yellow-Shafted
Flicker
090

Cerulean Warbler
091

Chestnut-Sided
Warbler
092

Pileated Woodpecker
093

Brown Thrasher
094

Roseate Spoonbill
095

Great Gray Owl
096

Egyptian Vulture
097

Harpy
Eagle
098

Ferruginous
Hawk
099

Common
Black Hawk
100

Red Kite
101

African Wood Owl
102

Red-Tailed
Hawk
103

Barred Owl
104

Barn Owl
105

Short-Eared Owl
106

Prairie Falcon
107

Swainson's Hawk
108

Snowy Owl
109

Turkey Vulture
110

Eastern
Screech Owl
111

Andean Condor
112

Burrowing Owl
113

American
Swallow-Tailed Kite
114

White-Tailed Eagle
115

Elf Owl
116

Imperial
Eagle
117

Osprey
118

American
Kestrel
119

Peregrine
Falcon
120

Snail Kite
121

Bald
Eagle
122

Northern
Goshawk
123

Merlin
124

Griffon Vulture
125

Long-Crested
Hawk Eagle
126

Golden Eagle
127

Northern
Harrier
128

Northern
Saw-Whet
Owl
129

Bateleur
130

Crested
Caracara

131

Great
Horned Owl
132

Sharp-Shinned
Hawk
133

African
Harrier Hawk
134

Gray Hawk
135

Gyrfalcon
136

Lämmergeier
137

Yellow-Shafted
Flicker
138

Cactus Wren
139

Common Loon
140

Mountain
Bluebird
141

142

Hawaiian Goose or Néné

Lark Bunting
143

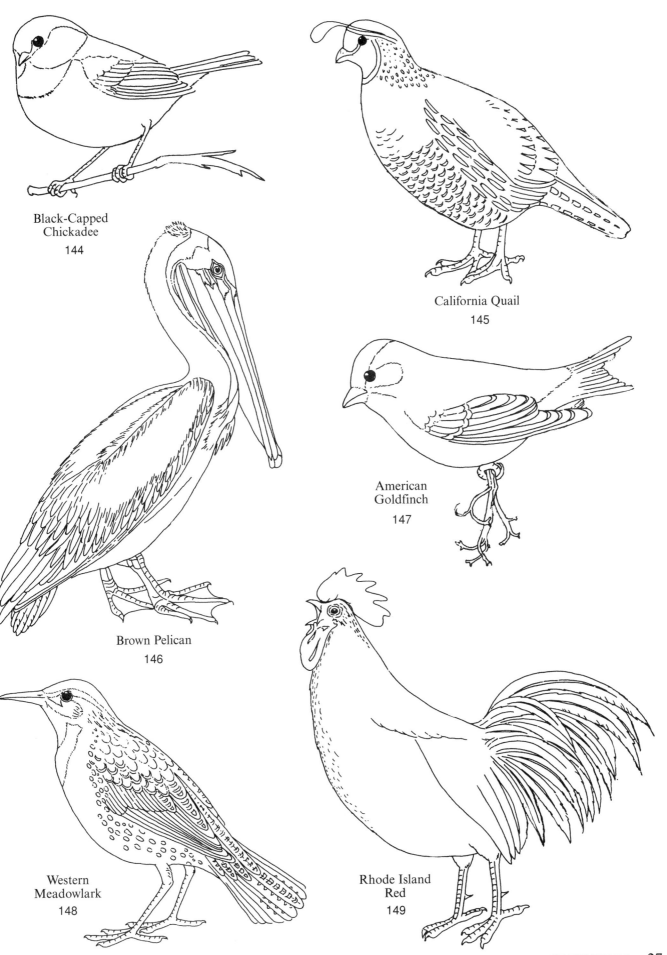

Black-Capped
Chickadee
144

California Quail
145

Brown Pelican
146

American
Goldfinch
147

Western
Meadowlark
148

Rhode Island
Red
149

Willow
Ptarmigan
150

Northern
Cardinal
151

Greater
Roadrunner
153

Baltimore
Oriole
152

Bald Eagle
155

Ruffed Grouse
154

Purple
Finch
156

Scissor-Tailed
Flycatcher
157

Carolina
Wren
158

Hermit
Thrush
159

American
Robin
160

Eastern Bluebird
161

Ring-Necked
Pheasant
163

Blue Hen
Chicken
162

Brown
Thrasher
164

Northern
Mockingbird
165

California
Gull
166

30   STATE BIRDS

Polynesian
Chicken
167

Hawaiian Owl
168

White Tern
170

Crested Honeycreeper
169

Hawaiian
Gallinule
171

Hawaiian
Hawk
172

Northern
Cardinal
173

Hawaiian
Flycatcher
174

Hawaiian
Coot
175

Oahu 'O'o
176

177

White-Tailed
Tropicbird

Red-Footed
Booby
178

Yellow-Green
Honeycreeper
179

Great
Frigatebird
180

Common Myna
181

Laysan Albatross
182

Hawaiian Crow
183

Hawaiian
Stilt
184

Hawaiian
Honeycreeper
185

'I'iwi
186

Hawaiian
Honeycreeper
(small, Kauai variety)
187

Palila
188

Hawaiian Duck
189

190

Scarlet
Hawaiian
Honeycreeper

Hawaiian Goose
or Néné
191

Herring Gull
192

Piping Plover
193

Magnificent Frigatebird
194

Dunlin
195

American
Avocet
197

Great Auk
196

Black-Necked Stilt

Ruddy Turnstone
198

Wood
Stork
199

Long-Billed Curlew
200

Atlantic
Puffin
201

202

Least Sandpiper

Common Snipe
203

Roseate Spoonbill
204

Purple Gallinule
205

Virginia Rail
206

Hooded Merganser
207

Northern Gannet
208

Spectacled Eider
209

American Oystercatcher
210

Black-Browed
Albatross
212

Peregrine
Falcon
211

Adelie Penguin
214

Long-Tailed
Jaeger
213

Limpkin
215

Wilson's Phalarope
216

American Coot
217

Trumpeter
Swan
218

Belted
Kingfisher
219

Double-Crested
Cormorant
220

Great
Egret
221

Brown Pelican
222

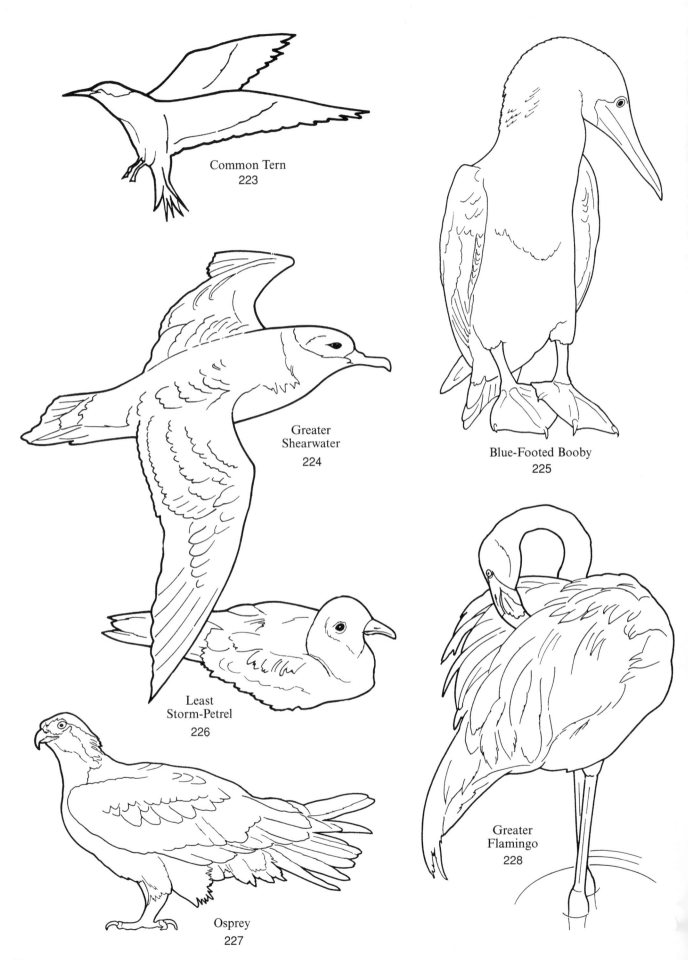

Common Tern
223

Blue-Footed Booby
225

Greater
Shearwater
224

Least
Storm-Petrel
226

Greater
Flamingo
228

Osprey
227

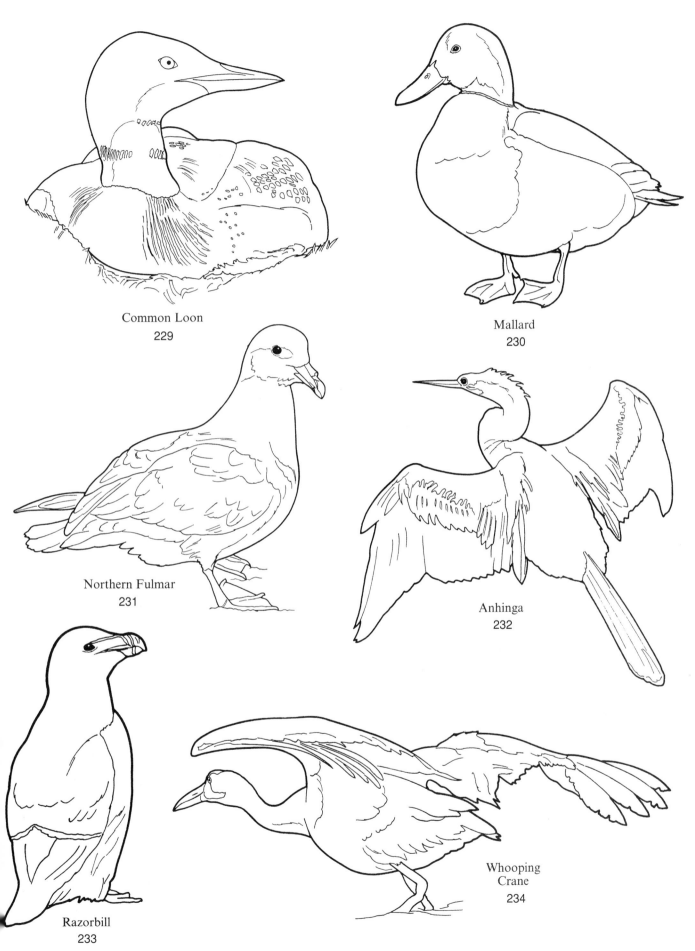

Common Loon
229

Mallard
230

Northern Fulmar
231

Anhinga
232

Razorbill
233

Whooping
Crane
234

Chinstrap Penguin
235

Adelie Penguin
236

Gentoo Penguin
237

Arctic Tern
238

239

Emperor Goose

Rockhopper Penguin
240

Atlantic
Puffin
241

Gyrfalcon
242

Black-Browed Albatross
243

Snowy Owl
244

Black
Guillemot
246

Willow Ptarmigan
245

Emperor Penguin
247

Skua
248

Parasitic Jaeger
249

Wilson's
Storm-Petrel
250

King Eider
251

King
Penguin
252

Lapland
Longspur
253

Steller's Eider
254

Wood Duck
255

King Eider
256

Mallard
257

Emperor
Goose
258

Barrow's Goldeneye
259

White-Winged Scoter
260

Snow
Goose
261

Ross'
Goose
262

Lesser
Scaup
263

264

Hooded Merganser

Greater
White-Fronted
Goose
265

Ring-Necked Duck
266

Common
Merganser
267

Tundra Swan
268

Surf
Scoter
269

Fulvous Whistling-Duck
270

271

Green-Winged Teal

Common Loon
273

Black-Bellied
Whistling-Duck
272

Spectacled Eider
274

Ruddy Duck
276

275

Canada
Goose

Cinnamon Teal
277

Brant
278

Canvasback
279

Blue-Winged
Teal
280

Oldsquaw
281

American Wigeon
282

Mute Swan
283

Common
Shelduck
284

American Black Duck
285

Bufflehead
286

Gadwall
287

Red-Breasted
Merganser
288

Barnacle
Goose
289

Common Eider
291

Northern Gannet
290

Harlequin Duck
293

Greater Scaup
292

295

Redhead
294

Trumpeter Swan

Pileated
Woodpecker
296

Roseate Spoonbill
297

Common
Yellowthroat
298

Wood Stork
299

300

King Rail

Green Heron
301

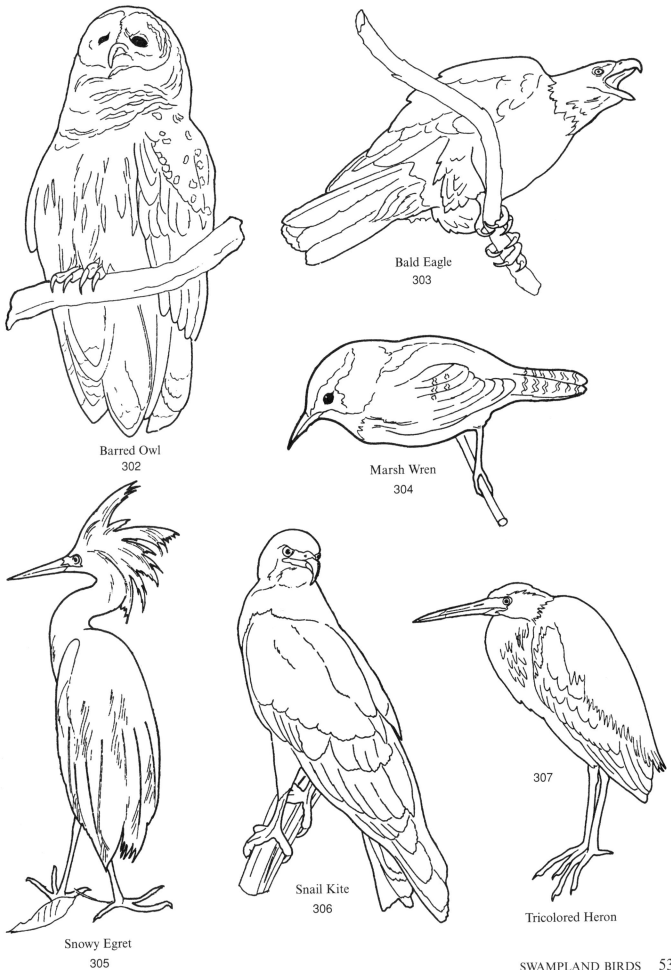

Barred Owl
302

Bald Eagle
303

Marsh Wren
304

Snowy Egret
305

Snail Kite
306

307

Tricolored Heron

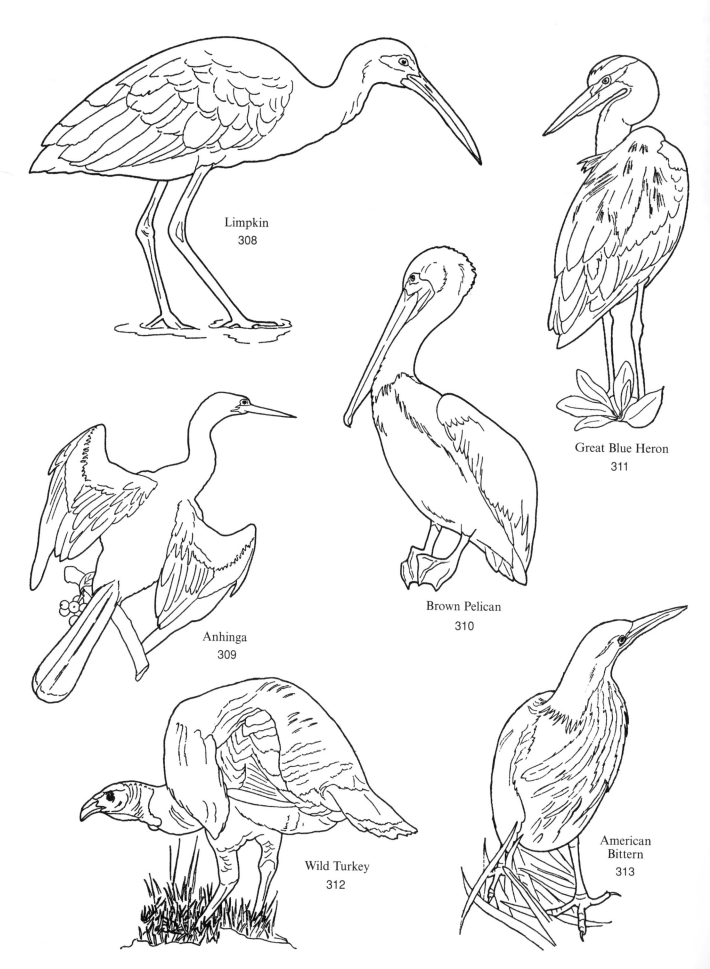

Limpkin
308

Great Blue Heron
311

Anhinga
309

Brown Pelican
310

Wild Turkey
312

American
Bittern
313

Satin
Bowerbird
315

'I'iwi
314

Garnet Pitta
317

Keel-Billed
Toucan
316

Green
Magpie
318

Mandarin Duck
319

Black-Eared
Golden Tanager
320

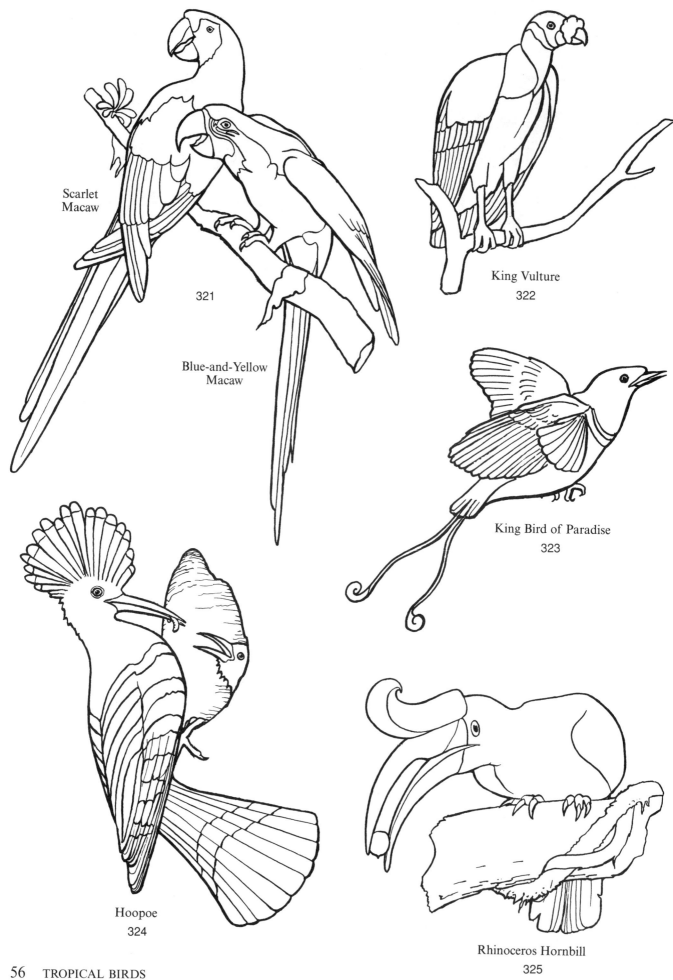

Scarlet
Macaw

321

Blue-and-Yellow
Macaw

King Vulture
322

King Bird of Paradise
323

Hoopoe
324

Rhinoceros Hornbill
325

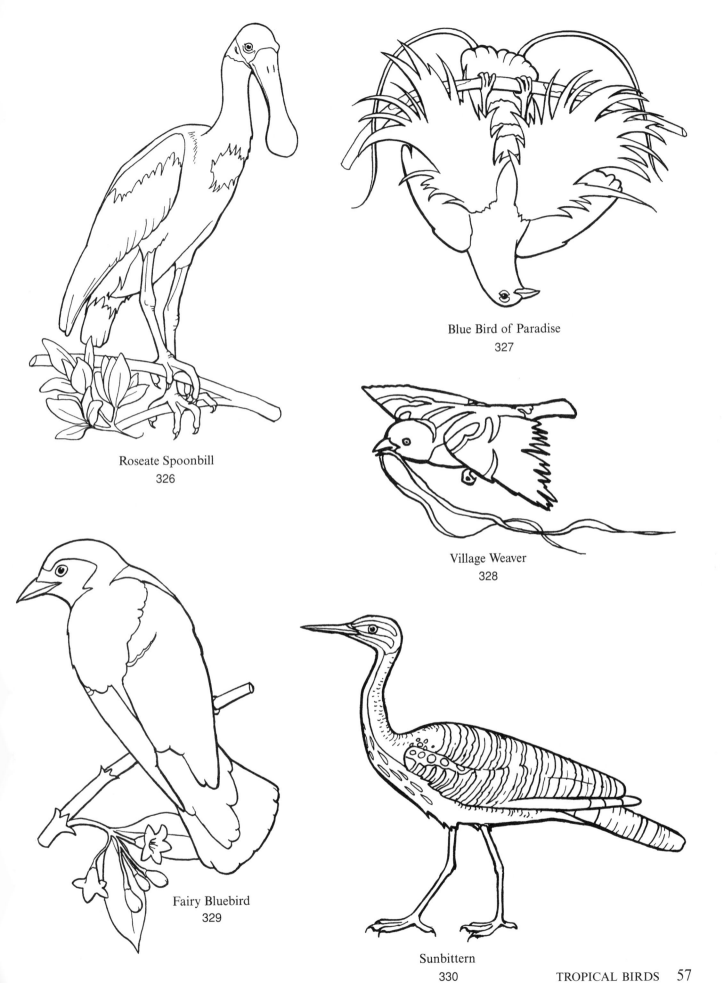

Roseate Spoonbill
326

Blue Bird of Paradise
327

Village Weaver
328

Fairy Bluebird
329

Sunbittern
330

Rufous-Breasted
Wren
331

Pink-Breasted
Paradise
Kingfisher
332

Copper-Rumped
Hummingbird
333

Emerald
Toucanet
334

Red-Collared
Lorikeet
335

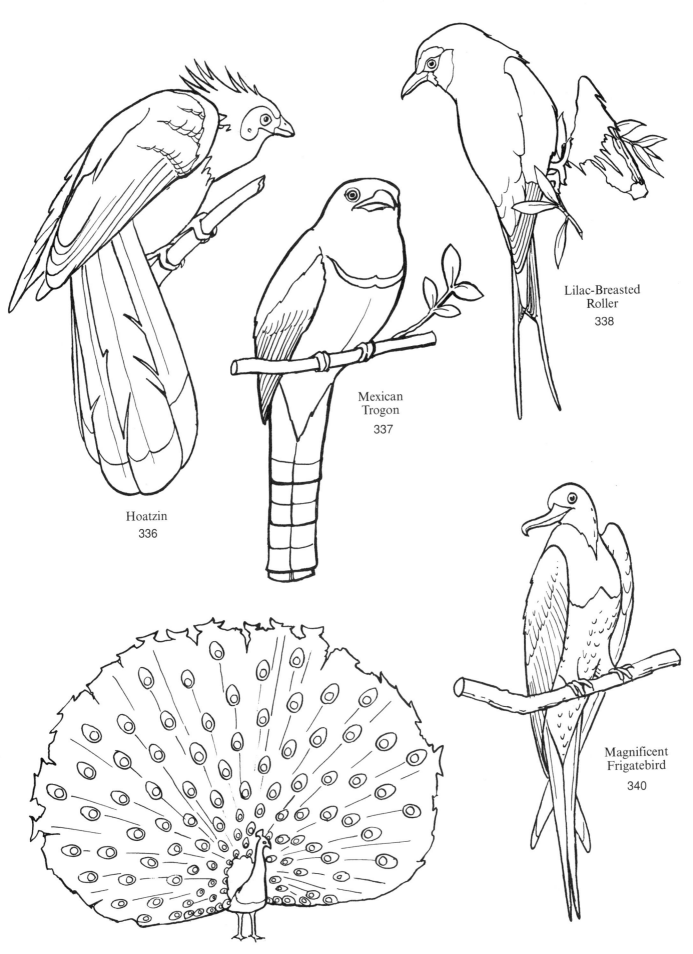

Lilac-Breasted
Roller
338

Mexican
Trogon
337

Hoatzin
336

Magnificent
Frigatebird
340

Common Peafowl
339

Greater Bird of Paradise
342

Green-Tailed Sylph
341

Regal Sunbird
343

Turquoise-Browed
Motmot
345

Cock-of-the-Rock
344

Tawny Frogmouth
346

Green Jay
347

White-Crested
Guan
348

Superb Lyrebird
349

Sulfur-Crested
Cockatoo
350

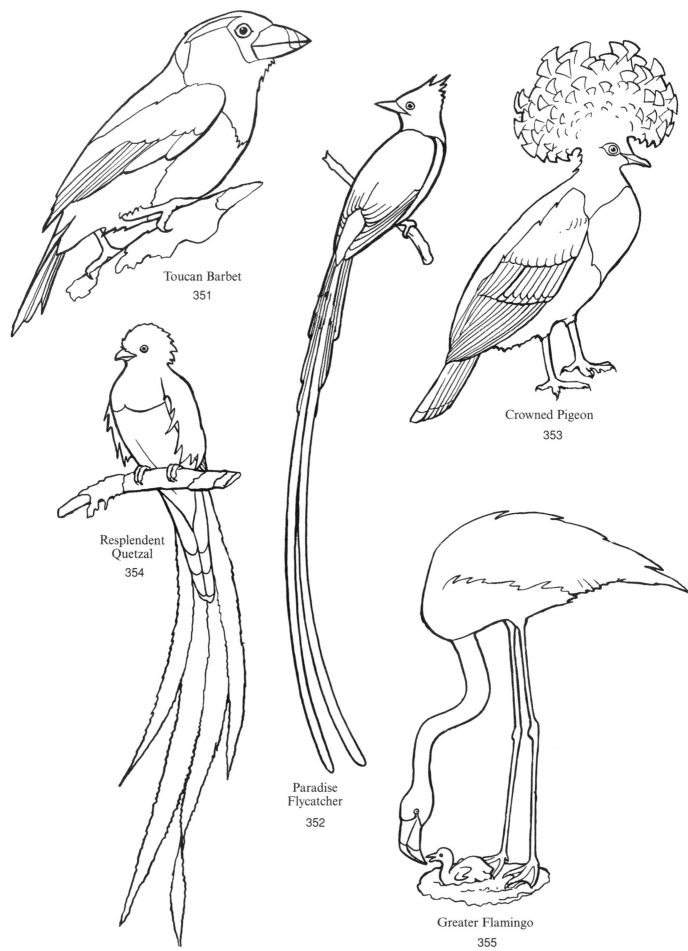

Toucan Barbet
351

Crowned Pigeon
353

Resplendent
Quetzal
354

Paradise
Flycatcher
352

Greater Flamingo
355

Common
Pheasant
356

Wood Duck
357

Herring Gull
358

Bank Swallow
359

Osprey
360

Black-Capped
Chickadee
361

Red-Tailed Hawk
362

Canada Goose
363

Piping Plover
364

Northern Harrier
365

Mute
Swan
366

367

Yellow Warbler

Herring Gull
368

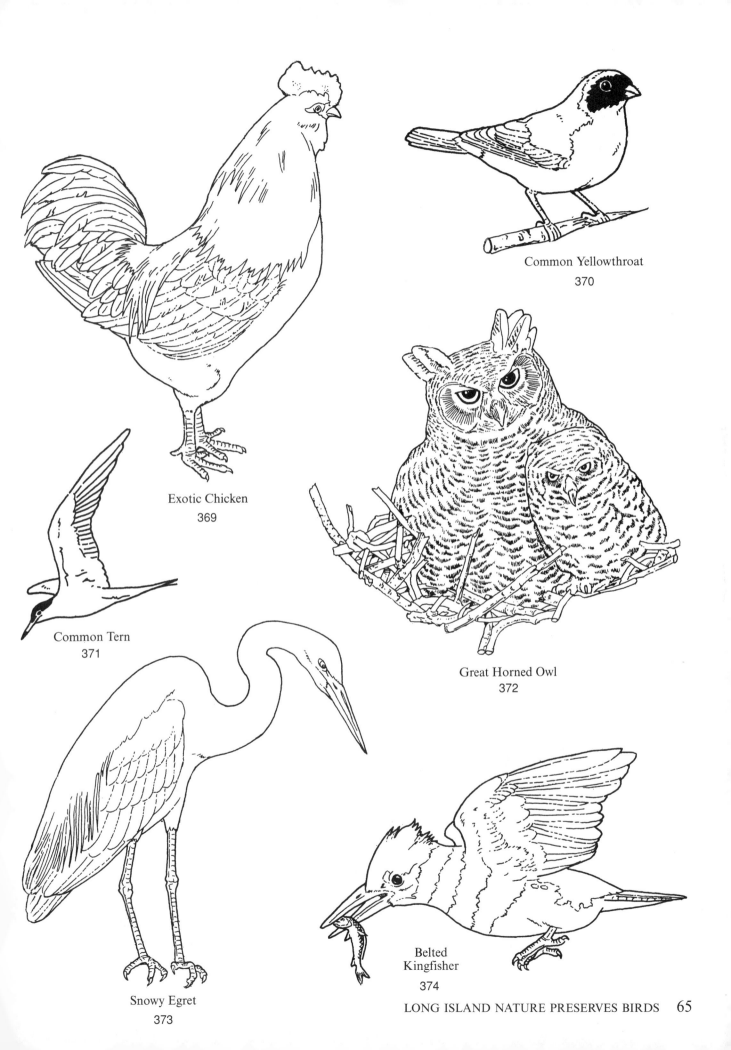

Common Yellowthroat
370

Exotic Chicken
369

Common Tern
371

Great Horned Owl
372

Snowy Egret
373

Belted
Kingfisher
374

Long-Eared Owl
375

Hyacinthine Macaw
376

Shoebill
377

American Crow
378

379

Helmeted Guineafowl

Turkey Vulture

380

White-Tipped
Sicklebill
381

Marabou
Stork
382

Kookaburra
383

Tawny
Frogmouth
384

Glossy
Ibis
386

Common Teal
385

Burrowing
Owl
387

Chickadee
388

Harpy Eagle
389

White-Headed
Vulture
390

California Quail
391

392

Golden Eagle

Cuvier
Toucan
393

Brown
Violet-Eared
Hummingbird
394

Western
Bluebird
395

Downy
Woodpecker
396

Great Hornbill
397

Ostrich
398

Gila Woodpecker
399

Northern
Cardinal
400

House Sparrow
401

Northern
Cardinal
402

White-Throated
Sparrow
403

Northern Carmine
Bee-Eater
404

Kori
Bustard
405

Ruby-Throated
Hummingbird
406

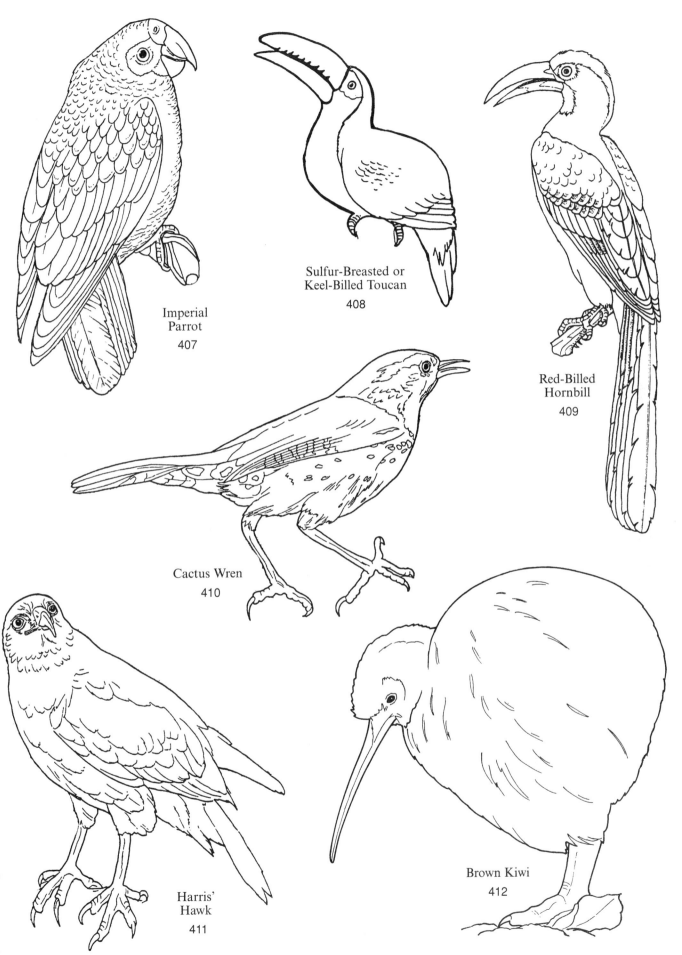

Imperial
Parrot
407

Sulfur-Breasted or
Keel-Billed Toucan
408

Red-Billed
Hornbill
409

Cactus Wren
410

Harris'
Hawk
411

Brown Kiwi
412

Baltimore or
Northern
Oriole
413

Northern
Mockingbird
414

Bee
Hummingbird
415

Buffon's
Macaw
416

Common Grackle
417

Secretary
Bird
418

Cedar
Waxwing
419

Index to the Birds